The Sassy Way to

KINDLE Bestseller Publishing

~~~

when you have NO CLUE…

by Gundi Gabrielle

First Edition Paperback: March 2017

ISBN-13: 978-1544875064
ISBN-10: 1544875061

The Cataloging-In-Publication Data is on file with the Library of Congress.

This is a **SassyZenGirl** *Guide*

FREE Bonus

Hi there!

Great to meet you! - I am excited to help you publish your first Amazon Bestseller!

To help you keep track of all the many tasks you need to complete during the next 30 Days, I prepared a "Bestseller Checklist", organized by week, to help you stay on target.

To access, just enter the following url:

SassyZenGirl.com/Bestseller-Checklist

Enjoy!
Gundi Gabrielle

TABLE OF CONTENTS

CHAPTER 1 - Write a Bestseller in 30 Days - 9

CHAPTER 2 - The 30 Day Plan - 19

CHAPTER 3 - How much does is cost…? - 24

CHAPTER 4 - WEEK 1 - 30

* Bestselling Book Ideas - 30
* The Amazon Algorithm - 40
* Research & Outline your Book Idea - 57
* Schedule Promos - 64
* Build your Launch Team - 78

CHAPTER 5 - WEEK 2 - 91

* Write your Book - 91

CHAPTER 6 - WEEK 3 - 96

* Find a Good Editor - 96
* Craft an Awesome Title & Subtitle - 99
* Find a Great Cover Designer - 103
* Build your Author Website - 107
* Final Edits & Formatting - 116

CHAPTER 7 - WEEK 4: Pre-Launch - 120

* Upload your Book to KDP - 120
* Your Author Central Page - 152
* Finalize Promos & Reviews - 154

CHAPTER 8 - Launch Week - 157

CHAPTER 9 - Post-Launch - 163

* What's next…? - 163
* Add a Print version - 167
* Add an Audio version - 169
* Further Training - 171

Final Words - 173

Chapter 1 - Write a Bestseller in 30 Days!

Sound crazy….?

Well…..actually, it isn't.

In fact, it is absolutely possible - and you can do it, too!

Why can I say that with such certainty?

Well… for one, because all my previous 6 books became not just bestsellers, but #1 Bestsellers, so I know a thing or two about marketing and how the Amazon algorithm works….;-)

And two, because we are not talking about bestsellers in the entire Amazon store, not even the entire Amazon Kindle store, but bestsellers in categories and sub categories!

Hmmm.....

You might have heard of the New York Times Bestseller list?

And, guess what.....there, too, bestsellers are listed in genres and sub-genres, just like music charts are sorted by style - Rock, Pop, Country, Classical....and further sub genres.

The difference is that there are a LOT more categories on Amazon, therefore, a lot more chances to be a bestseller in one of them.

In fact, if you follow the strategies in this book - and that includes ALL of them, especially, the first part - topic research - it will be very hard for you *not* to have a bestseller!

That's right!

Take that in for a moment…..

and look at this beautiful picture….3 of my books in the Top 5 of Marketing:

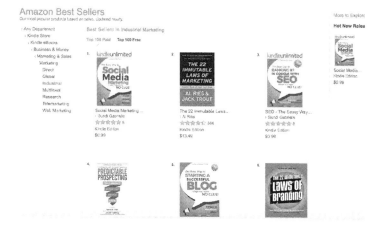

Now imagine your own books there....

Good feeling?

Hold that image as you read this book and for the next 30 days as you are writing your first bestseller.

BUT......

You say.

There are so many BUTs why this can't possibly work for you:

- You are not a writer
- You don't know anything about marketing
- You don't have a list of ardent followers
- You don't know what to write about
- You are not tech savvy
- It just won't work
- You need a publisher
- You need luck

Anything else....?

Well...

I have an answer for all of them, but first, I'd like to make a bold suggestion:

How about, you ignore all your BUTs for the next 30 days?

Seriously!

Just for kicks....

Bury them. Ignore them. Not interested!

Would it change anything for the worse?

If so, what?

What exactly would be worse, if you didn't listen to your BUTs for once?

Sorry, for the "motivational speech", but this is holding back so many people with wonderful talents that I need to address it at least once.

From what I can see, it's like this:

You listen to your BUTs and they will convince you that's it not worth to even try.

So you do nothing.

Least risk, I guess. But also no progress, no success - nothing...

On the other hand, you ignore your BUTs and just trust the process...

What's the worst that could happen?

* You might not succeed
* Your friends and family might laugh at you for thinking you could do it
* You lost a few hundred dollars in production and promo expenses (we'll keep expenses to a minimum in this book)
* Your self-esteem suffers

Ok, those are not fun. Understandable.

But would it be the end of the world?

I mean, really?

Probably not.

In fact, you would have learned and explored so many new things - and *passionately* pursued something that had been your dream for a long time.

You finally did it. You finally know what it's like. It's out of your system and your life will never be the same again.

Isn't that alone worth giving it a shot?

Like I said before - if you follow the steps in this book, especially the part about researching your topic - you will have to try very hard *not* to succeed - even if you are not a writer, know nothing about marketing and have no ardent readership yet.

So, how about giving your BUTs a 30 day vacation and instead use all that formidable energy to write your first bestseller?

How about it?

While you contemplate that...;-) - let me share how I got started:

*Please note, for the print version I created a **Resources Page** with all direct links mentioned in this book (usually in bold). Just open it now and keep it available while you read:*

SassyZenGirl.com/Kindle-Resources

In the fall of 2015, I became a member of **Location Rebel** an online community of Digital Nomads and those who wanted to become location independent through running an online business they could access from anywhere in the world.

Awesome courses and community, btw, if you ever want to **check it out**.

Part of the course was a webinar with **Lise Cartwright**, another Location Rebel member, who had published several #1 Amazon Bestsellers.

In the webinar, she showed us how she did it in clear, simple steps. I watched the video several times and then got to work, applying every step exactly as she had taught - and 4 weeks later, I had my first #1 Bestseller!

The steps she taught weren't unique.

They were pretty much the same methods every successful Kindle author uses, and they are shared once again in this book.

If I can do it - so can you!

Really!

Are you ready?

Ready to see your book at #1, ahead of big names like "Lonely Planet" and "Eat, Pray, Love"? This is my **Bali Guide from the Zen Traveller series**:

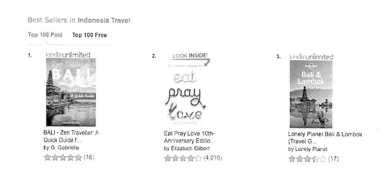

That sure was an awesome feeling, and the Bali book is still selling really well, especially in paperback.

However, it's not just a great feeling. Being able to call yourself a "Bestselling Author" comes with additional benefits that will affect your entire business and online presence:

- The *Prestige* of being a Bestselling Author
- You establish yourself as an *Authority* in your field
- It will be great *(free) PR* for whatever business or service you are offering
- Kindle Publishing is a great list builder and one of the easiest and fastest ways to *build an online following* for your blog, your social media and/or your business.

Amazon actually *pays* you to get all these things - and that brings me to another point:

- Kindle can be become a wonderful ever growing *passive income stream*, especially if you go beyond just one book and also add print and audio (more on that later).

There is really no reason *not* to write a book and take on this new adventure!

So…..if you are ready…..

Lets get started!

Chapter 2 - The 30 Day Plan

The first important step for any successful strategy is mapping out an:

ACTION PLAN

Without a plan you don't know where you are going - and you certainly don't know how to get there.

The following is an overview of all the tasks you need to complete over the next 4 weeks. Adjust time frames as needed - (60 days instead of 30 etc) - depending on how much time you can devote every day.

As a minimum, you should have 2-3 hours every day to make any significant progress.

More is better, obviously.

If it helps, you can download the Bestseller Checklist offered in the beginning of this book - or you can write your own, based on the below.

SassyZenGirl.com/Bestseller-Checklist

Now, lets have a look:

WEEK 1 - Preparation & Research
- Research Profitable Book Topics
- Keyword & Category Research
- Content Research for your Book
- Write an Outline
- Schedule Launch week Promos
- Build a Launch Team

WEEK 2 - Write
- Write your Book

WEEK 3 - Fine Tune
- Find a good Editor
- Send your Draft to Test Readers/Reviewers
- Craft an AWEsome Title & Subtitle
- Order a GREAT Cover
- Set up your Author Website
- Final Edits & Proofreading
- Format your Book

WEEK 4 - Prelaunch

- Upload your Book to Amazon
- Forward your Book URL and ASIN to Promo sites
- Add Book URL to Review Request Page & Website
- Schedule Reviewers
- Write a compelling Book Description
- Fine tune Category Research
- Set up your Author Central Page

That's it!

Whoa…..wait!

You say.

Just 1 week for writing an entire book?

That's crazy! - And I'm so busy. I will need at least several months!

Ok - lets clear something up: when it comes to ebooks:

"Short is the new Long"

as successful author and book marketer Penny Sansevieri writes **in her awesome book "Sell Books by the Truckload"**.

That means, readers prefer shorter books when reading online or on digital devices.

Short books do a LOT better on Kindle than full length 60-80K word books. Fiction writers say that their short novellas tend to be much more popular than big, long novels, though there is certainly a place for those as well.

12K-24K words is a good range on Kindle. More, feels overwhelming to many readers, because the way we read on a digital device is different than holding a book in your hand.

It's more effective to split a complex topic - or novel - into a series of smaller books, than overwhelming your readers with one, big, huge one.

It's also better from a marketing perspective.

Authors who generate a 5 to 6 figure income from Kindle Publishing, usually have a series of books covering different aspects of an overall topic. Actually, most of the time, they have *several* series in different genres (often under different pen names).

Not to get carried away, but to give you a larger perspective....

Writing 12,000 words in 1 week is not difficult - even if you are not an experienced writer. That's about 2000 words a day - a good size blog post.

And....if you want to give yourself more room on your first book, by all means, plan in 2 weeks - or more - just not more than a month.

It's important to have a deadline to keep yourself focused.

Now, take a moment and write out your Action plan. No worries, you can always adjust along the way, but you need a clear plan and make a firm commitment before you start.

Once you are done - sign and date your Action plan and hang it on the wall above your desk.

Now, you are ready to go....;-)

Chapter 3 - How much does it cost...?

Let's start with the good news:

Self publishing is surprisingly inexpensive!

In fact, it is free to publish your Kindle book on Amazon and your paperback through Createspace, Amazon's print-on-demand outlet.

Print-on-demand is a great option, especially for new authors, because you don't have to pre-pay 1000 books and store them in your garage. Instead, a book is only printed when someone orders one.

The production price per book tends to be a little higher than with mass production, but given that you never pay or advance any money - that in fact, you *get* paid a royalty when someone buys your book, this is of little concern, unless you start selling thousands of books every month.

— > Cost of Publishing on Amazon: FREE

MANDATORY EXPENSES

The 3 areas you should invest in - if you want your book to be successful that is - are:

1) A GREAT cover
Do NOT even think about creating one yourself. Your cover is your business card. It needs to look professional and will be one of the most important factors determining your book's success. More on that in the next chapter.

— > Cost of a GREAT Cover: $100-300

2) A good Editor
Many 1 star reviews come from readers frustrated with bad formatting and constant typos. You don't want to provide unnecessary "ammunition" and it's impossible to do yourself.

Editing has 2 parts: **Content Editing** and **Proof Reading**. As a minimum you should hire a proof reader.

— > Cost of Editing - depending on word count - $150-300

3) Launch Week Promos

Unless you already have a large following, you will need some promos to get the ball rolling and trigger the Amazon Algorithm to market your book.

There are a wide range of promos available at very different price ranges, and we'll cover them in Week 1. As a minimum you should budget $100. $200-300 if you can - but $100 can work if you are on a tight budget.

— > Cost of Promos: Minimum $100

Again, the above numbers are estimates to give you an overview and also depend on your book's length.

Counting it all together, you could - at an absolute minimum - publish your first book for just $400, though I recommend having a little more room, also for promotions.

— > TOTAL Minimum Required Budget: $400

OPTIONAL EXPENSES

Formatting

If you are not very tech savvy, you might have to outsource the formatting of your book. The writing softwares can take care of it nicely - if - there are no complicated graphics etc.

And if it still doesn't come out right, there are many inexpensive gigs on **Fiverr** to help you along.

Market Research

I will mention two softwares in the next chapter that will make the all important initial research a LOT easier and faster. They are priced at $47 and $97 respectively.

Again, these are optional, but they are an immense time saver and can complete elaborate research in just a few minutes, that would otherwise take you hours, if not days to complete manually.

Proper topic and keyword research can dramatically increase your income and long term success, and is *the* most important part of your planning stage.

Writing Software

Will be covered in the next chapter. Again not required, but a good option long term if you plan on writing a lot of books. Cost would be $45.

Otherwise, Microsoft Word will be perfectly fine for your first book.

Author Website

You should definitely have one - and a self hosted one - so you can place landing pages etc. (will explain in the pre-launch chapter).

Costs is $10 for a domain name (annual fee) and a monthly fee of less than $5 (I have a discount offer for you at just $3.49 in the pre-launch chapter).

Easily Access Amazon's Top Reviewers

You will need a lot of reviews to trigger Amazon's algorithm. Beyond just asking people you know, you also want to contact the top reviewers on Amazon and get them to review your book.

You do NOT pay them - that would be a violation of Amazon's policies and could get you banned - but there are softwares that make the process of finding the reviewers most suited for your book a LOT faster.

This can start a $25 for a month (you can cancel at any time).

That's pretty much it!

Chapter 4 - WEEK 1

Bestselling Book Ideas

A little warning….

This will be the most extensive and complex chapter. Please don't let that prevent you from reading all the way through - even if it feels a little overwhelming the first time.

The information in this chapter will make or break the success of your book.

Without this research, without an understanding of how the Amazon algorithm works and how people find your books, you will not achieve long term success - let alone bestseller status.

So, take a deep breath…….and let's dive right in!

What it takes to publish a Bestseller on Amazon

The most important part of this entire strategy is research: finding a book topic that sells.

You need 2 ingredients:

- a large interested readership = a topic that people actually *want* to read about

- medium to low competition = as an example: you wouldn't be able to compete with 10 New York Times Bestselling authors in the same category

How to research?

Let's start with the Kindle bestseller lists. **This Youtube video will visually take you through the process -** use time stamps 1:02-10:40

see Resource Page:
SassyZenGirl.com/Kindle-Resources

To find Kindle Bestseller lists, click on "Kindle eBooks", then "Best Sellers":

Next, select a genre (= category) that might interest you. If you already have an idea for a book topic, this method can help you validate or fine tune.

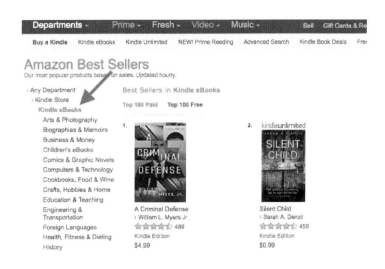

As a new author, you will usually not rank in the overall categories, but you *can* rank in the sub categories.

Go through a few and find out what themes are trending. Focus mostly on the top 20 and see if certain topics show up at least 3 times.

If yes, then this is a topic readers love. As a new author you don't want to reinvent the wheel, but rather follow trends that have already proven to work, — > that are making other authors money.

While you go through the lists, also check the Sales Rank for books #1, #10 and #20.

Here is how:

Click on each book, scroll down to "Product Details" and find the Sales rank. It's called "Amazon Best Sellers Rank" and shows where each book ranks within the entire Kindle store (all genres included):

Product Details

File Size: 3388 KB
Print Length: 382 pages
Page Numbers Source ISBN: 1503943429
Publisher: Thomas & Mercer (April 1, 2017)
Publication Date: April 1, 2017
Sold by: Amazon Digital Services LLC
Language: English
ASIN: B01KXQ8S96
Text-to-Speech: Enabled
X-Ray: Enabled
Word Wise: Enabled
Lending: Not Enabled
Screen Reader: Supported
Enhanced Typesetting: Enabled
Amazon Best Sellers Rank: #1 Paid in Kindle Store (See Top 100 Paid in Kindle Store)
    #1 in Kindle Store > Kindle eBooks > Mystery, Thriller & Suspense > Thrillers > Legal
    #1 in Books > Mystery, Thriller & Suspense > Thrillers & Suspense > Crime > Murder

Why?

Because the Sales Rank of a book can give you a rough idea of how well that particular book is selling. There are no exact numbers, of course, but in general, anything over 100,000 is rarely selling a copy at all.

Anything under 1,000 is selling like hot cakes. Even under 10,000 sales are very impressive. Above 30,000, sales begin to slow down.

Ideally, you are looking for the following metrics within the top 20 books of each sub-genre:

- No more than 3 books under 10,000 (otherwise, too competitive)

- No more than 10 books over 30,000 (otherwise, not enough sales, not a popular category)

You don't have to hit these numbers exactly, but just to give you a basis to work with.

To make this a lot faster and time efficient, I recommend a Chrome browser extension named **"KindleSpy"**.

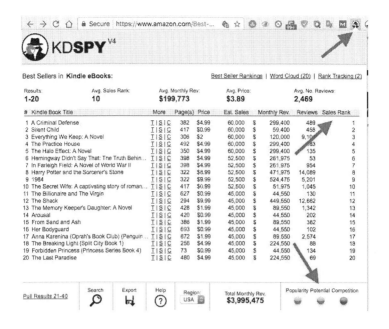

Best Sellers in **Kindle eBooks**:

Best Seller Rankings | Word Cloud (20) | Rank Tracking (2)

Results: 1-20	Avg. Sales Rank: 10				Avg. Monthly Rev: $199,773		Avg. Price: $3.89		Avg. No. Reviews: 2,469	

#	Kindle Book Title	More	Page(s)	Price	Est. Sales	Monthly Rev.	Reviews	Sales Rank
1	A Criminal Defense	T | S | C	382	$4.99	60,000	$ 299,400	489	1
2	Silent Child	T | S | C	417	$0.99	60,000	$ 59,400	458	2
3	Everything We Keep: A Novel	T | S | C	306	$2	60,000	$ 120,000	9,100	3
4	The Practice House	T | S | C	492	$4.99	60,000	$ 299,400	83	4
5	The Halo Effect: A Novel	T | S | C	350	$4.99	60,000	$ 299,400	135	5
6	Hemingway Didn't Say That: The Truth Behin...	T | S | C	398	$4.99	52,500	$ 261,975	53	6
7	In Farleigh Field: A Novel of World War II	T | S | C	398	$4.99	52,500	$ 261,975	954	7
8	Harry Potter and the Sorcerer's Stone	T | S | C	322	$8.99	52,500	$ 471,975	14,089	8
9	1984	T | S | C	322	$9.99	52,500	$ 524,475	5,201	9
10	The Secret Wife: A captivating story of roman...	T | S | C	417	$0.99	52,500	$ 51,975	1,045	10
11	The Billionaire and The Virgin	T | S | C	627	$0.99	45,000	$ 44,550	130	11
12	The Shack	T | S | C	294	$9.99	45,000	$ 449,550	12,662	12
13	The Memory Keeper's Daughter: A Novel	T | S | C	428	$1.99	45,000	$ 89,550	1,342	13
14	Arousal	T | S | C	420	$0.99	45,000	$ 44,550	202	14
15	From Sand and Ash	T | S | C	386	$1.99	45,000	$ 89,550	382	15
16	Her Bodyguard	T | S | C	693	$0.99	45,000	$ 44,550	102	16
17	Anna Karenina (Oprah's Book Club) (Penguin ...	T | S | C	872	$1.99	45,000	$ 89,550	2,574	17
18	The Breaking Light (Split City Book 1)	T | S | C	256	$4.99	45,000	$ 224,550	88	18
19	Forbidden Princess (Princess Series Book 4)	T | S | C	73	$0.99	45,000	$ 44,550	134	19
20	The Last Paradise	T | S | C	480	$4.99	45,000	$ 224,550	69	20

Pull Results 21-40

Search Export Help Region: USA

Total Monthly Rev. **$3,995,475**

Popularity Potential Competition

This nifty little tool shows you all the above numbers at the click of a button!

You can breeze through tedious research that would otherwise take you hours, in just a few minutes.

KindleSpy also gives you scores for competition and popularity.

Another very helpful feature is "Word Cloud". We'll talk about that in the Keyword chapter.

KindleSpy costs only $47, works on both Mac and PC, and is used by pretty much every bestselling author I know.

Don't worry, I always like to run all my projects on minimal expenses, but these are the two research tools I strongly recommend:

- **KindleSpy** for category and market research (you can see it in action in the above video)

- **KindleRocket** for keyword research

Both make life so much easier and can really help you increase your earnings by positioning your book in the most effective categories with the highest converting keywords. KindleRocket is scheduled to become a monthly subscription in the not too distant future, so **best get it while it's still a one-time fee**.

.....especially, if you plan on writing more than one book.....

And why wouldn't you?

Publishing gets easier and smoother with every book you write. And more fun, too!

Coming back to research though….

Whether manually or with **KindleSpy**, repeat the above process with every single sub category that could even remotely be of interest as a book topic. Also use the "Look Inside" feature in the top books and browse through reviews.

Customer reviews can be a gold mine of information. In particular, negative reviews, because they tell you what readers want to see, e.g. what was lacking in a book or could have been explained more in-depth, etc.

See if you notice trends: What readers enjoyed and were satisfied with. What they were actually looking for in that particular type of book, and where you can see an opportunity to improve or niche down.

What are their problems, pain and frustrations that you could help alleviate?

Once you've gone through all possible categories, you should have a list of candidates with numbers to tell you whether that topic is popular, marketable and not too competitive.

Sleep on it for a night and then make a decision. If possible, find a topic that lends itself to a series, exploring different aspects in each book.

For example, the **"Successful Blog" series** that you are reading starts with the **technical aspects of how to set up a blog or website**. Next come the first important steps you need to take to grow a following. From many reader emails I knew what challenges they were facing and how some felt stuck.

Hence **the 2nd book,** which covers the basics of internet marketing and growing an audience.

The final 3 books cover the main strategies of internet marketing:

- **SEO**
- **Social Media**
- **Kindle** (most people don't think of Kindle in this context, but I found it to be the fastest and easiest way to grow a following and establish an online presence).

Future books can include Affiliate Marketing, Copywriting and many other areas. All in the same style and geared towards the same audience.

Once people like your style and find benefit and value in your books, they will likely buy more than just one and even become enthusiastic test readers when you need **reviewers** for your next book.

Always keep that long term aspect in mind. You don't *have* to write a series, but why close the door from the start? You might actually like the idea later on…..

Now let's go over Amazon's algorithm. It's crucial that you understand how it works and what you need to do to get in front of as many readers as possible.

The Amazon Algorithm

To start, let's understand that Amazon is a search engine - not unlike Google or Youtube.

That means, most potential readers will find you by entering a search phrase - a "keyword" - into the search bar, and your book will hopefully show up in the top spots.

That's the #1 method.

Here are some more ways readers can find you - if they don't know your name or book title already, which is unlikely when you are new:

#2 - by browsing the bestseller lists of specific categories

#3 - by browsing the "New & Popular" pages of specific categories

#4 - by seeing your book under "Customer's also Bought" (on a related book's page)

Customers who bought this item also bought

59 Seconds: Think a Little,
Change a Lot
› Richard Wiseman
★★★★☆ 179

Managing Oneself (Harvard
Business Review Classics)
Peter Ferdinand...
★★★★★ 474

The Millionaire Real Estate
Agent
› Gary Keller
★★★★☆ 556

#5 - in an ad at the bottom of a related books page

#6 - through a Google Search

#7 - in a Facebook ad. That's right! - Amazon actually invests money to promote top selling books. You might have seen some in your timeline already.

#8 - in an email from Amazon with book recommendations based on your past purchase and browsing history

Ideally, you want to show up in all of the above, but different criteria apply for each.

Bestseller vs. Popularity

You might be surprised that "Bestseller" and "Popularity" are not the same when it comes to Amazon's algorithm.

A **Bestseller** is determined solely by sale's rank, e.g. how many books you sell per day.

Simple.

Popularity on the other hand, is a combination of several factors:

1) Sales Rank
How many books you sell

2) Relevance
This is where "keywords" come into play. The search phrases a potential reader will enter into the search bar to find book suggestions.

You need to optimize your book listing in such a way that Amazon understands what it's about and where to place you.

You could call this "Amazon SEO" (Search Engine Optimization).

Related to this is "Bounce Rate":

How readers respond when they click on your book after finding it in the search results. Do they stay and read your book page? (Description, reviews, etc.)?

Even better, do they buy your book?

Or - do they click back to the search results - and how quickly?

"Bounce rate" is a marketing term and also applies to Google, Youtube and other search engines.

It is the strongest indicator for Amazon to know whether customers find your book *relevant* for that keyword. Based on that feedback, Amazon will rank you -> your popularity score.

3) Price
Amazon is all about making money - and lots of it! - Generally, higher priced books get preference. Once again - *not* in the bestseller rankings, *only* for the popularity score.

Lower priced books usually sell more copies, but overall, might still make less than a higher priced popular book.

This does *not* mean you should price your book as high as possible - quite the opposite! - It's just one additional factor in the algorithm to be aware of.

4) Social Proof

On Amazon, social proof comes first and foremost through the number - and average rating - of your books reviews. It is one of *the* most important ranking factors and something you should continually strive to increase.

5) Sales Velocity

How consistently your book sells. A quick spike through an effective promo might get you to bestseller status - and even to #1 - but unless you keep those sales numbers high, your popularity in Amazon's eyes will drop quickly.

Amazon wants to see consistently high sales and an organic rise, rather than a sudden splash.

Of course, you should still do a number of powerful promotions during launch week to get the ball rolling, (don't worry, they are not expensive and easy to set up), but understand, that it's only meant to help you get to bestseller status - and - to get noticed by Amazon's algorithm, so they will use their huge marketing power to promote you.

We'll cover points 1 and 3-5 in the pre-launch chapter, but for now let's focus on "relevance".

How can you "optimize" your book for Amazon's ranking algorithm?

Step 1: find keywords that:
- customers use a lot = **high search volume**
- have **low competition** = not too many other books are trying to rank for the exact same phrase

Similar to selecting a winning book topic or categories, right?

Frankly, similar to ranking in Google (SEO) or any other search engine (Youtube, Pinterest, etc.)

Step 2: optimize your book's "meta data" (title, description, reviews) for those keywords, so Amazon understands what your book is about and should rank for.

Just like Google, Amazon's search engine employs "bots" to crawl the site and each page on it - continuously. The purpose is to catalogue all meta data for each book and make them available to the algorithm for ranking purposes.

So, it's not human beings completing this enormous task. You are training bots and you need to send signals that the bots can understand.

Let's look at each step in detail:

To find ideal keywords, you can start by entering a word or two in the search bar. The keywords you are looking for are called "Long Tail Keywords", phrases of 3 or more words.

Why?

Because they are more specific and less people are competing for that exact phrase, making it easier to rank - especially in Google, which can be an additional great traffic source.

When you enter, don't complete the phrase. Instead watch what suggestions Amazon comes up with:

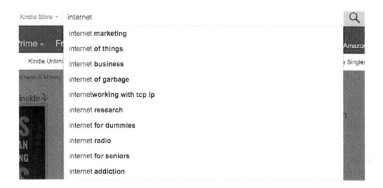

All those phrases are popular keywords, meaning keywords that users have frequently entered into the search bar.

To get even more detail, you can add a word, followed by the letter 'a' - or in the below example 'm' - and let Amazon autocomplete with a number of variations:

Go through the whole alphabet. Yes, even x, y, z…..

Write down any keyword that could be relevant to your book topic. You should have quite a list at the end - all of them popular.

Now you need to determine how competitive they are.

For each keyword you want to check:

1) Number of books per search term. You can find that number here:

2) How many books have the *exact* keyword phrase in the title or subtitle. The less books, the easier it will be to rank for that specific keyword, just like in regular SEO

3) Sales Rank of the top 10 books

Once again, this process is greatly accelerated by using **KindleSpy**, especially when you go through a lot of keywords, but you can also check each book page manually.

In addition, KindleSpy's "Word Cloud" function can show you what keywords are most frequently used by the top ranked books.

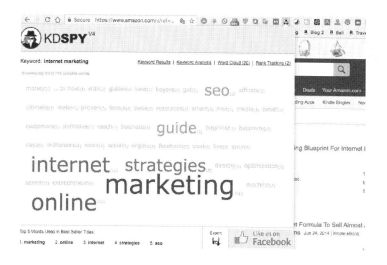

The numbers from the previous chapter once again apply.

A much faster way to find winning keywords is a software called **Kindle Rocket**.

Rather than spending hours on all the above, Kindle Rocket can give you results in just a few minutes, scouting *both* Amazon and Google and providing you with scores for competitiveness.

You want to find about 15 applicable keywords, so you can swap them as needed. Over time, some keywords might not work as well anymore, so it's good to have a range of options.

Keep in mind that the choice of keywords can have an enormous influence on your sales - and therefore long term income.

Books have been known to go from just a few sales per day to several hundred, just by changing keywords. That's how powerful and important this step is!

Kindle Rocket costs $97, but will soon go to a monthly subscription, so best grab it while it's still a one-time fee.

Optimizing your Book Page

Once you have picked your keywords, you need to place them in such a way that Amazon will show your book in the top 3 (at least top 5) whenever someone enters those phrases.

Here is how (to be completed in Week 4, but we'll cover the steps now, so you understand how this all works and ties in together):

Add your chosen keywords to your book's meta data:

1) Title & Subtitle
THE most important place for your *main* keyword is your title - ideally at the very beginning.

Then, add a few more keywords in the subtitle. You might have noticed that especially in non-fiction, sub titles are usually quite long.

Pay close attention from now on, and you will notice relevant keywords sprinkled throughout that subtitle.

If you write fiction, you can still place relevant keywords in title and subtitle while keeping your artistic flow.

Look at the difference - before and after:

The Haunted Grounds: (Jack Tapper Series)

vs.

The Haunted Grounds: a Mystery Thriller Novel (Jack Tapper Action Thriller Series)

Notice how you naturally added the very relevant and popular keywords "Mystery Thriller", "Novel" and "Action Thriller"?

People search for those phrases to find new books to read, so include them as much as possible without overstuffing.

For fiction books there is also the option to replace a few keywords with "themes".

Themes are grouped into:

Moods - Characters - Settings

You can check out a few Amazon themes on the Resources page:

Romance Themes

Mystery, Thriller and Suspense Themes

Science Fiction & Fantasy Themes

Here is a complete list.

2) Description

Your book description is immensely important and we'll cover descriptions in more detail in the Pre-launch chapter.

For SEO purposes - as it relates to this chapter - you want to sprinkle all your keywords throughout the text. For fiction, also include your chosen themes.

You want your description to be around 500 words (longer is ok).

Why?

Because Amazon and Google bots will not take notice of your description under a certain minimum length. Ranking will then be that much more difficult.

3) Editorial & Customer Reviews

Yes, that's right. If reviewers happen to mention relevant keywords in their review, it also triggers the algorithm and helps with ranking.

If all this still seems a little overwhelming and strange, I suggest reading **book #3 of this series**, which covers in detail the principles of SEO and search engine ranking. It's an easy 2 hour read and will help you with your website and social media ranking as well.

Now, let's come back to our initial list of 8 ways that potential readers can find you:

- As we already mentioned, Bestseller lists are determined solely by Sale's Rank, e.g. how many books you sell.

- Amazon and Facebook ads are bought by customers and publishers to market their books.

Amazon runs ads, too, including on Facebook, and you can probably guess which books they will choose to promote?

That's right: the ones with the highest "popularity score".

- Same goes for "New & Popular" and "Customers also Bought" as well as the book recommendation emails that Amazon sends out.

- When readers enter a keyword into the search engine, it is once again the popularity score that determines who shows up first.

What about Google ranking?

For Google, it's mostly how well you optimize your book page. Google does not have access to your sales figures or other internal parameters. Google bots will only crawl your book page and make a determination based on what they find.

Amazon is one of the most popular sites in the world and therefore has one of the highest Domain authorities - DA - (see **SEO book**), making it much easier for your book to rank on page 1 than say, your brand new website that starts with a DA of 0.

Finding the right keywords and then optimizing your book's meta data - title, description, reviews - will make or break the long term success of your book, so be sure to spend a good amount of time on this research.

Research & Outline your Book Idea

Phew…..

That was a pretty brainy chapter…..

Time for a breather!

Fortunately, this was the most complex part of your preparation. Now we get to actually *writing* your book.

Ready?

Then, here is the next step:

Once you have decided on a sellable topic, you can spend the rest of the week doing all the necessary background research and writing an outline for your book.

You probably have a good knowledge of your topic already. At least for your first book, that would be recommendable. But even if you don't, you can easily research LOTs of awesome information online through blogs, relevant Youtube channels, and other Kindle books - and then turn it into a book.

If you are good at explaining things in an easy-to-understand, entertaining manner, you will do your readers a great service - even - if you are *not* an expert on the topic.

After all, you are saving them many hours of doing all that research themselves and crystallize it into a 1-2 hour read.

As long as you do your research well, and your facts are accurate and come from highly regarded sources, your content will be valuable and helpful.

Obviously, you shouldn't copy anybody's words or ideas. You would quickly get in trouble for copyright violation - plus, it's unethical.

But by reading a lot about a topic - and from a number of different sources - you will gather a good, solid understanding that you can then transfer into your own words and structure.

You may also occasionally need to do this in a book series, when one of the topics is not your specialty, but still important for the whole series.

Remember, you are not writing a dissertation or a scientific paper. For most non-fiction you give how-to advice to regular people who are often beginners in that field.

You need to have a good, solid understanding of the topic and be well read and researched on all relevant areas, but with beginner guides, you don't have to be the absolute, #1 top expert. You just have to be good at explaining things and know whatever you write about really well.

Of course, be ethical about it and do your homework. Aim to provide as much value as you possibly can, but don't be intimidated if you find a topic that you would really like to write about or a niche that you've always wanted to explore.

Many successful, bestselling non-fiction authors started that way.

If they weren't experts, they *became* experts by reading up and learning as much as they possibly could about the subject and then presented it in a fun, easy to understand way that readers enjoyed and got great value from.

Especially, when your professional background is not in a field that would lend itself to profitable book ideas, you might have to branch out and explore new areas to become an expert in.

If you do it well and apply the marketing principles taught here, the financial rewards will certainly make it worth your while.

These next few days then are about collecting as much information as possible. Anything you will need to properly - and expertly - write your book.

Write an Outline of your Book

To add some structure to your writing week, start with an outline of your book.

It's pretty easy:

First, write out the main chapters and sub chapters.

Then add bullets under each sub chapter, listing all relevant talking points you intend to cover.

Don't write it out yet and keep moving things around as needed. Make sure it flows well.

You can use cork boards for chapters and bullet points, or outline on a piece of paper or in a word document.

There is also a special writing software that most long term authors use, but you do *not* - repeat - *not* need that for your first book.

If your budget is tight, definitely leave this one out.

You can write your book in Microsoft Word and then export as a Word document or ePub. Many authors do it that way and it's perfectly sufficient.

In case you are interested - or maybe for future reference - the software I'm talking about is **Scrivener,** available for both Mac and PC, and people also use it to write their Master's thesis or other scientific papers.

Scrivener offers a cork board feature which is really helpful for brain storming and outlining a book.

This is what it looks like:

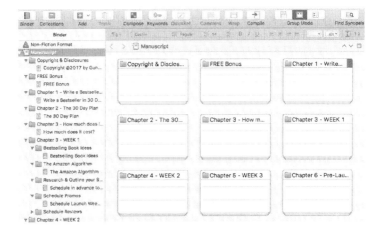

The cool thing is, that you can instantly switch those cork boards to document mode and then continue to write your manuscript right from there, basically just fleshing out the bullet points.

No need to transfer anything.

Another feature, that's really helpful and saves time, is the chapter layout.

Each chapter and sub chapter is its own separate entity until the final compiling stage, so you can easily move them around without copy/paste and having to scroll up and down endlessly.

You can also easily add additional sub points or chapters wherever you need without messing up your entire formatting.

It's really quite amazing.

Once again though, if your budget is tight and you just want to write this one book, MS Word will do just fine.

Schedule Promos

For launch week you should schedule a few promotions to get the ball rolling and help readers find your book.

Once you enroll in KDP Select (see pre launch week), you are allowed to schedule two types of promotions: Free & 99c

Let's first understand how the KDP royalty structure works:

- Kindle Books priced less than $2.99 or higher than $9.99 get a royalty rate of 35%.

- Kindle Books between $2.99 and $9.99 receive 70% royalty on all sales.

Amazon also deducts a few cents for delivery depending on file size, but it's a minimal amount.

$2.99 is the most widely used Kindle price, $3.99 can also work well depending on the topic, but anything over $5 usually doesn't sell well - if at all.

Readers expect Kindle books to be priced in a certain range, and if you go above, they tend to look elsewhere.

This does not apply to famous authors or big publisher brands, of course, but for an unknown, self-publishing author - especially, a brand new author with no following - it's best to stay within trusted price ranges and first get some steady momentum going, before starting to experiment.

Make sense?

The Power of "Free"

"Free" is one of the most influential power words in the English language and a free offer is almost irresistible to most readers.

Yes, there will be a few who only pick it up because it's free, but so what..?

You haven't lost anything! - It's not a physical book with production costs. Once it's uploaded, it doesn't cost you a dime - not even when someone downloads for free - so be generous, until you have a solid audience - and that will take a little while.

Instead, focus on the enormous exposure a free promo can give you. Thousands of new readers who would otherwise never hear about you or your book!

Self-published books are a dime a dozen - there are actually 1 Billion ebooks on Amazon!

So give new readers the easiest possible way to find and get to know you. If your book is good and provides value to their lives, they will recommend you to their friends and co-workers. They might even leave you a review (and those are hard to come by….).

You might even gain an enthusiastic, lifelong fan, just because you were generous once! That's worth *much* more in the long run than a quick buck through selling at regular price - *if* you even make a sale…..

Plus, a high number of downloads will kick Amazon's algorithm into gear, resulting in heavy promotion of your book through searches, "Hot New Releases", "Also bought" etc.

With your first book, your main concern should not be to make as much money as possible, but rather to attract as many new readers as possible.

You need publicity more than anything else and nothing is more powerful PR than the word "FREE".

Should you do a free promo with every book you publish?

Not necessarily. I don't do them much anymore, but I also have a large readership and mailing list now. I still occasionally run one for a day or two, especially if a book is slagging and could use an extra punch.

Or - if my main goal is list building and driving traffic to my site or business. So it's not all just about sales...

How to Schedule your Promos?

Please note, that these recommendations are for the English speaking market and in particular, the US store.

If you write in another language, google "Kindle book Promos", see what is available in your country and try them out or see what author forums in your country recommend. Those are often a gold mine of information and hot tips!

Most promos are inexpensive, so you are not losing much if you try a few, and there won't be that many choices in other languages and countries.

If you are aiming for the US market, I would recommend the following sequence. I mention them in Week 1, because most promos need to be booked ahead of time and while some will not accept you until you have a book link - or, in some cases, a minimum of 5-10 reviews - you should still contact them now and see if you can get on their calendar.

You don't want to leave it all to the last moment...

1) The FREE Promo Phase

Kindle Select allows you up to 5 days where you can set the price to "Free".

2-3 days is usually enough. After that, downloads tend to slack off and it's better to take the momentum into the next promo stage: 99c

As I already pointed out, there are two Bestseller lists on Amazon: one for free books and one for paid.

Sales rank from "Free", does *not* carry over to "Paid". However, the momentum, the buzz and activity a free promo generates, *does* affect how Amazon views your book and how much they are willing to promote you.

2) The 99c Promo Phase

99c promos can be run indefinitely, but for your first book, I would do 3-5 days - with a different promo each day - and then switch to regular price, e.g. $2.99 or whatever you chose.

The best days to publish free books seem to be Sunday and Monday according to several studies and the direct experience of many authors. Monday through Wednesday are ideal for 99c promos - even Thursday is still pretty good. The two days to avoid are Friday and Saturday, unless you schedule promos for an entire week.

Let's look at this in action:

1) Your official book launch is Sunday and you start with a FREE promo for 2 days - Sunday and Monday

2) Tuesday through Thursday you run several 99c promos and Thursday evening you switch to $2.99 or whatever your regular price is. It will take a few hours until the system updates.

What to do for Promo Days?

Aside from telling everyone you know and spreading the word on your social media, mailing list etc., you want to schedule your book with a number of promo services.

Most of these services have accumulated large mailing lists - or Facebook groups - of passionate readers and send out daily emails with new book deals - both free and 99c.

Some of these services are free (and usually not that effective), others charge a fee.

Their effectiveness varies greatly and on the Resources Page you can find **a listing of 127+ promo services** that you can use.

I have found only a few to be really worth the money, so will be sharing my personal favorites here. (Please note - I'm not getting a commission or discount for recommending them).

These are the ones I used to get my first two books to #1 Bestseller status and thousands of downloads in the first week alone. They are all highly regarded among authors:

FREE PROMOs

Books Butterfly

Not cheap, but absolutely worth it! THE best free promo service around with an active daily readership of several hundred thousand(!) and a guaranteed number of downloads (usually in the thousands), otherwise, they will refund you on a pro-rated basis.

Every single time I used this promo, I had several thousand downloads in just one day.

What's more, they will honestly tell you *before* you pay, if your book will fly with their audience, and recommend the package that's most realistic. It has nothing to do with you or your book personally - they won't read it - but they know from experience what topics work with their audience - and how well.

I would book this promo on the last Free day and start with a few lighter ones to build up momentum.

You might remember sales velocity. When scheduling promos it is best to start with the slowest (=least effective) and then build up to the strongest, so you have an organic, steady increase in sales/downloads which is what the Amazon algorithm loves. This goes for both free and paid.

James Mayfield

The other service I can highly recommend is James Mayfield. He is an author himself, a really nice guy, and runs an awesome social media promo, placing your free book in front of 500,000 Facebook users spread over 10 groups, as well as a number of other social networks for just - get this! - $13 !!

Yep, that's right! - Amazing price.

If you do nothing else, but just James on day 1 and Books Butterfly on Day 2 for your free promo days, you should have a solid number of downloads and hold the #1 spot in multiple categories for the FREE lists! Obviously, no guarantees. All this very much depends on your topic, an awesome cover and a few excellent reviews, but if you have those 3 in place, plus the above 2 promos, your book should be doing *very* well.

See direct links to all Promos on the Resources Page.

99c PROMOS

My two top recommendations for 99c promos are:

Buckbooks

They are the best (aside from Bookbub - see later) and I always get great results with them. Paid downloads will obviously be a lot less than free, but unless you pick a super competitive Amazon category, this promo alone should easily carry you to bestseller status - if you are not already there - and possibly even #1.

It's always done that for me. In the case of **my Bali book** even beating out "Lonely Planet" and the top international Bestseller turned Hollywood movie "Eat, Pray, Love" - all this for just $29 buck!

It's quite difficult to get into Buckbooks though. They have high quality standards and require a superb cover (no self-made or cheap Fiverr job) and a minimum of 10 reviews.

As a newbie, your best chance of getting in, is by ordering your book cover through their sister company **100Covers**.

They are specialized on Kindle covers and start at only $100 (which is as low as you can get for a professionally designed cover), so a pretty good deal for both a great cover and this excellent promotion (when your book is not even finished).

For your second book, you can use a different cover designer. Once they know you, you can always book more promos, but as a newbie and first timer, this is the easiest - and often only way - to get on their calendar.

Buckbooks should be the last day of your 99c promo and then use that momentum to switch to regular price.

BKnight

A Fiverr gig, but a *superb* one that pretty much every bestselling author recommends. At only $5 bucks you will get some nice early sales - and if you are not happy with the results, they will gladly refund you. Really awesome guys and always very accommodating.

Even last minute requests or changes are usually possible.

For 5 bucks, you will be featured on their high traffic website for a day. For an additional 5 bucks they will also add your book to their daily email newsletter (which I would recommend).

Fussy Librarian
Cute name and another good service, but usually booked up for at least a month. They offer both free and 99c at just $12-14 for 1 category and $20 for 2, also very reasonable.

Bookbub
The Goldstar among promo services, but also the most expensive - several hundred dollars per promo - and most difficult to get into. They don't usually accept brand new books, but want to see how a book

is doing over time: number and quality of reviews, sales numbers, ranking etc.

They will also check your book for expert editing and formatting - and even then, there is no guarantee.

If you *do* get accepted, the number of possible downloads and sales is enormous - **you can see average figures here, sorted by genre**.

Definitely, keep Bookbub in mind for future promos, just not for launch week.

KindleROI

This is another Chrome extension by the creator of KindleSpy, allowing you to schedule most of the free available promos with just the click of a button. "Free" here means promo services that don't charge you.

You can either submit to each service manually - one by one - which can take a few hours. Or - with this tool - simply open your book page in Amazon and click on the extension button.

A window will open, with your meta data already filled in. You simply add your email address, pick whether you want a FREE or 99c promo, enter the dates and click submit.

Takes about a minute - versus many hours, doing the same thing manually.

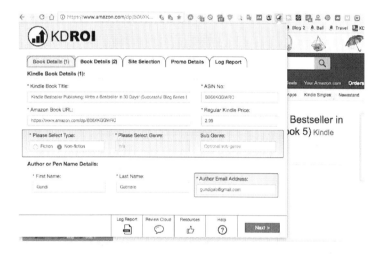

You can get KindleROI here.

FKTB

Very effective promo with hundreds of thousands of readers, mostly women over 40. Offers a "New Release" option - even if you don't have reviews yet - but is very specific on what topics and genres they accept.

Build a Launch Team

During this first week you also want to send out emails and Facebook posts, inviting people to become a test reader and reviewer in return for a free copy of your book (in pdf format).

Ideally, you want to find people that are interested or have expertise in your book topic and you should not include close family or friends as that is against Amazon's strict reviewer policies.

Why do you need reviewers?

2 reasons:

1) You want to get objective feedback on your book *before* you publish.

How it flows, is everything clear, areas that aren't properly covered and explained etc.
Ask them to be honest and not sugar coat anything. This can be incredibly helpful, especially if you don't hire a content editor.

2) You will need at least 5 reviews (ideally more) on or around launch day.

Why?

Because as we already saw, reviews matter greatly to Amazon's algorithm, providing social proof and factoring *greatly* into your popularity score.

Secondly, buyers will hesitate to purchase a book or product without any reviews. It just looks iffy, not trustworthy, and no one wants to be the first to buy or leave a review.

Thirdly, most good promo services won't accept you without a minimum number of reviews. At least 5, often actually a minimum of 10.

This is why you need to send emails and social media posts during week 1 and ask people to commit to the following:

- Read your book and give feedback by the middle of week 3
- Download your book on Amazon during week 4 - pre-launch week - and leave a review on or before launch day.

We'll go over how to set that up later.

- They need to confirm that they have an active Amazon account with past purchases of at least $50, or they won't be allowed to leave a review due to Amazon's strict reviewer rules.

Because reviews are so important, abuse of the system with floods of fake or purchased reviews had been rampant and demanding this minimum threshold for reviewer eligibility is one way Amazon curtails unethical practices. Authors and sellers used to have multiple accounts under different names with the sole purpose of leaving themselves 5-star reviews.

You could even buy Fiverr gigs that placed reviews from fake accounts *for* you, so Amazon's response is not over the top, but was very much needed.

They also check every single review manually within a few weeks.

If there is any indication that reviewer and author are close friends or related - again a violation of reviewer guidelines - that review will removed.

If two reviews come from the same IP address - or even worse from the same IP address as the author - they will all be removed.

Authors swapping reviews is not permitted either. Of course, if you really want to read each other's books and leave a genuine, objective review, that would be ok, but the lines are blurry and author review exchanges are explicitly forbidden.

All of this is meant to protect the consumer - all of us - who rely on genuine reviews for our purchase decisions. While it may be frustrating as a new author, there is a good reason for all these restrictions, and they protect us all.

Inviting people to review your book and offering a free reviewer copy is certainly permitted, even encouraged by Amazon, as they want a lot of reviews on each book page. Just do it within the guidelines and never, ever purchase reviews - or you might find your account suspended one day and all your books deleted.

It's just not worth the risk.

Reviewer Instructions:

Once you have a good list of interested reviewers, send them an email and thank them for their interest. Let them know when you will be sending them your manuscript (as a pdf attachment) and be very clear - repeat it several times - on the deadline by which they need to give you feedback and a second deadline by which they will have to leave a review (your launch day).

Be aware that not everyone will follow through. They all mean well and are excited for you, but everyone is busy and life gets in the way. That's why you need to be crystal clear on your deadlines and that getting a free copy is *contingent* on them keeping those deadlines.

Still, not everyone who promises will actually deliver, so try to have *at least* 20-30 on your list to have a definite 5-10 reviews on launch day. The more, the better.

Explore forums and Facebook groups related to your field and ask for reviewers there. People are usually interested and happy to help out and you spread your net as wide as possible rather than focusing on your immediate friends and family.

People who naturally interested in your topic will also be much more eager to read your book and be more qualified to review it.

Guidelines for Reviews - VERY important!

Given Amazon's strictness and relentless removal of any reviews that violate their policies, you need to give your reviewers very clear guidelines.

Yes, ideally, you want wonderful, positive reviews, but hymns of praise with little substance or specific reference to your book are not helpful and even a little suspicious to other readers.

Reviews should be relevant and objective, with helpful, detailed information specific to the book - helping a buyer to decide whether this is the right book for them.

They should not address you personally - or even worse - thank you for the book. They can say "the author" or use your last name, but keep it objective and neutral.

Also, ask them to write at least a few lines, not just "Great book. Enjoyed it". Giving some examples of what they liked or how the book helped them. What their experience level is with the topic etc.

In that context, they can also mention a keyword or two where it fits naturally. The emphasis being on "naturally". Less is more. Once is enough.

Finally, they should first download the book from within their Amazon account and leave the review while logged in.

That way, it will count as a "verified" review. Those are reviews from people who actually purchased the book.

Yes, you can leave a review even without purchasing the product, though unverified reviews count a lot less and are less trustworthy in a customer's eye.

Do not ever ask for a specific rating or a 5-star rating. It's a violation of policies that can get your account suspended, plus it's unethical.

One important note:

If you live in the US and all your reviewers are also in the US you can ignore this point. If, however, you have an international audience, they will usually have to leave reviews on their country's page (Amazon UK, Amazon Germany, etc.) and the various country stores do not share reviews. Even the book pages look different.

Whatever your main store is, that's where you want most of your reviews, especially if it's the US store which is the most competitive by far.

3 More ways to get Reviews

1) Goodreads

Goodreads is a great social network for authors. Definitely one you should consider becoming quite active in and network. The platform is also owned by Amazon, so give it a try if you are not already a member. It's free to join.

Through your networking and participation in Goodreads groups, you can also ask people to leave a review for your book on Amazon (not just Goodreads) and quite a few will probably do so.

Goodreads in general, is a great platform to spread the word about your new books and make them available to interested readers.

2) Amazon Top Reviewers

One of the standard methods for increasing your review count is to contact "Amazon Top Reviewers".

You can find a link to their list on the Resources Page.

You want to find top reviewers that have reviewed books similar to yours, e.g. are interested in your field.

To find them you will need to browse through each profile to check what type of books - if any (some only review products) - they have reviewed in the past and then contact them via email to request a review.

Once again, this can be very tedious and time consuming when done manually. Instead you can join the **Author Marketing Club** - a great community with many different tools and features - and get access to their **Review Grabber function** which will filter out appropriate reviewers for you, complete with email address.

Then, all you have to do is contact them. Be sure, to look through their profiles and find something personal you can mention. Maybe you come from the same state, share a common interest, or they have a dog that you can refer to. The point is to stand out from the hundreds of generic cut + paste emails they receive every day and show them that you actually bothered to read their profile.

Mention similar books they have reviewed to explain why you think they might be interested in yours.

Keep it brief and personal - don't forget to address them by name - and let it go. Some will respond, some won't, but gradually your review count will go up and these will be quality reviews with the "Top Reviewer" badge next to the name, adding trustworthiness and weight.

3) Ask for a review at the end of your book

This is a big one! - Always, in every book, have a page at the end, asking your readers for a review with a direct link to your book.

The majority will still not do it, but even a slow, regular stream of new reviews will be helpful.

We'll get back to this during pre-launch.

Getting more reviews will be a continuous effort - long after your book has launched. For now you are only concerned to get a minimum of 5 reviews on launch day, try for more if possible. Definitely, aim for at least twice that number. It will always be less than you expect, even if people commit.

How to handle negative reviews

Everyone gets them and that's totally ok as long as good reviews by far outweigh a few negatives. In fact, your review profile will look a lot more trustworthy with a bit of a mix.

You still - very importantly - need to keep a vast majority of 5-star reviews and an overall average of ideally at least 4.5, definitely no less than 4.

Otherwise, new readers will balk.

Never attack a reviewer or try to argue with them. In most cases, I would ignore them and move on. The only time I would comment is if the review is very detailed and clearly misrepresenting your book. Those types of reviews can be hurtful and should be clarified.

In that case, thank the reviewer for the detailed feedback and even offer a refund since they weren't happy with your book.

Then calmly and politely, correct whatever was misstated, close by thanking them again and leave it.

Your response is not for the sake of that reviewer, but for others who might read it. They will watch carefully how you respond and how you handle criticism. Are you professional and polite about it or do you turn into a petulant crybaby? You can win over quite a few new readers if you handle this with grace and class - and even the reviewer themselves might be swayed by your response and change their mind. They don't get notified of your comment though, so don't expect too much....

Also, negative feedback when genuine can be helpful to you. We sometimes miss things, don't cover a certain sub topic enough - or it can even be a topic for a new book....

Not all bad review are created equal - and they are most certainly not the end of the world....;-)

Chapter 5 - WEEK 2:

Write Your Book

Week 2!!

Time to write your book - finally!!

Are you excited?

If you are an experienced writer and believe you "got this" - fire away.

If you would like some pointers, here they are:

#1 - Have a specific reader - an avatar - in mind and write as if you were having a conversation with them. More like blogging in other words.

It will be a much easier reading experience, especially on a digital device.

#2 - In that same line, don't do big blocks of text. Break it up with shorter paragraphs and frequent sub heads. *So* much more pleasant to read.

#3 - Do NOT write a title yet. That's a whole science in itself and will be done in week 3 while your manuscript is with the editor.

You also want to keep an open mind as to where the book is "going". Sometimes during the writing process, you may find a new angle or a new direction and you don't want to be constrained or limited by a finished title.

#4 - there is no "ideal" length for eBooks, except that, in general, shorter books do better than longer. For your first book, I would suggest staying under 24,000 words - even 10-12K is fine.

Less is more and top value content is more important than a huge word count.

#5 - in your first draft - just brain dump!

 Just write and write away. No editing, stopping, thinking, just let it flow.

If you start to edit while writing, you will never finish and it will interrupt your creative flow.

Just write....

Enjoy the process. Enjoy having it flow out of you.

If you properly researched and outlined your book, this should feel like one big release.

Letting all that information finally pour out on paper (digitally...;-)

If you are not an experienced writer and don't know how to start - STOP THINKING!

Just start writing, even if it's something silly or you think it's terrible grammar.

Nobody cares.

It's about getting started, open the floodgates and let it flow. Sometimes, this may take a day or two - and that's ok.

Don't panic, don't judge, just write - and write - and write......

With non-fiction, writer's block shouldn't be much of a problem. If you did your outline well, just follow those bullet points and do the best you can.

Before you start…

Use your outline to create a daily schedule with the chapters you want to complete each day.

Some will be more extensive than others, so spread the chapters out over 5 days as you deem most effective. Adjust accordingly if you gave yourself more than a week to write the book.

Then commit to fulfilling each daily tasks in the set time frame.

I say 5 days, so you have a buffer day should you need it and you will also need 1-2 days to re-read and correct your manuscript.

Once again - if 1 week is intimidating, schedule 2, or even a full month, but no more than that.

Otherwise, you'll never finish….;-)

Always save

Super important piece of advice!

Always save everything immediately, even as you are writing. Programs can occasionally freeze and shut down and you'll lose everything you wrote, if you don't constantly save as you write.

In addition, try to save your manuscript always in 2 places. If one gets lost, or accidentally deleted, you don't loose your entire manuscript. You can use a thumb drive, external hard drive, cloud account etc.

It happened to me once with my first book after it was already finished and published. Can't remember why, but it was suddenly gone - no manuscript left anywhere on my computer!

Fortunately, I was able to retrieve a pdf copy through my Createspace account where I had published my print version and could then copy and paste it back into Scrivener.

But without that virtual back up from an already published book, it would have all been gone forever - and you don't ever want that to happen!

Chapter 6 - WEEK 3

Find a Good Editor

Editing will be one of the 3 necessary expenses for any book launch, because a book with lots of spelling errors or bad grammar can get hit with some pretty nasty 1-star reviews, and could also be refused by the better promos who check for quality.

Editing falls into two areas:

- Content Editing: your writing, grammar, structure of the book etc.

- Proofreading

If your budget is tight and you feel you are a very experienced writer, you might skip on content editing, but you should definitely hire a professional proof reader.

Cost depends on the length of your book - word count - and editors charge either by hourly rate or flat fee.

I always insist on a flat fee with any freelancer I hire, because it encourages timely delivery and protects me from unexpected bill hikes. In fairness though, an editor should then be allowed to have a look at your manuscript first to see how much work is involved.

If there are a lot spelling errors, bad writing or grammar etc., it will obviously take them a lot longer to complete the job and they should be properly compensated.

It's very important that you are crystal clear on your deadline and that delays are not acceptable.

Of course, that also implies that you give them your manuscript on the agreed date and don't delay. Always, fairness both ways.

An easy way to find good editors is **Upwork**. You can post a job listing there, upload a sample page from your manuscript and ask interested candidates for a sample edit. That will give you a good idea of who might be a good fit.

I had excellent experiences with this service:

TheLanguageAgent.com

Fast, reliable, good prices, and absolutely trustworthy.

Archangel Ink is another good, though rather expensive option.

Craft an Awesome Title & Sub Title

Now that you've finished your manuscript, you can spend a few days crafting an awesome, attention grabbing title.

Don't take this lightly. It is an incredibly important step!

A great title will significantly increase click-through rate to your book. Click-through rate is a marketing term and describes how many people are enticed to click on your book's thumbnail to find out more.

Both, book cover and title, are the two important parameters here, which is why both need to be outstanding.

Crafting great titles is an art, and headline writers for the top magazines are among the highest paid writers in the world.

If this is new to you, I recommend spending a day, just reading the following fantastic articles to get a sense of what it's all about and what you need to focus on *(see direct links on the Resources Page)*:

The A-B-C-D Formula for Irresistible Non-Fiction Book Titles
Derek Doepker's comprehensive article

Four Strategies for Creating Titles that Jump Off the Page
from the master himself - Michael Hyatt

Headline Templates (not just for blogs, but also work great for books):

52 HEADLINE HACKS:
A Cheat Sheet for Writing Blog Post Titles that go Viral
The Classic - a Must Read!

100+ Blog Post Title Templates that Grab Attention
More great Title templates

Title Generator Tools:

These nifty free tools can be quite effective….and get your creative juices going *(links again on the Resources Page):*

Portent's Title Generator

Adazing Title Generator

A list of title generators for different fiction genres can be found on the Resources page.

❖❖❖❖❖❖❖

In case you thought it was just the title you had to "worry" about....

....the subtitle is just as important!

This article by the one and only Chandler Bolt teaches you what to focus on. *(Resources page)*

Use keywords in both Title and Sub Title

We already talked about this in the Keyword section. Place your main Keyword in the title, if possible, right at the beginning.

Sprinkle a few more keywords in the subtitle. You can also use keywords in the series name if you have one.

Use Polls to Test your Titles

The easiest - and free - way to hold a poll, is to ask your followers and friends on social media. Usually, they will gravitate to one vs. the other, and it also starts building curiosity about your book, especially when you ask people's opinion and let them participate in the process.

A very effective way on a larger scale - and more expensive - would be targeted Facebook Ads. There is a bit of a learning curve though, so maybe not ideal for your first book, but **here is a free course** that teaches you how to do it - the right way.

Another great tool is **PickFu**.

This (paid) platform allows you to run polls with targeted audiences and not only do you get a vote, but you will also get the reasons why people chose one over the other. Very importantly, these are people who don't know you and are therefore much more objective and resembling a typical reader - more than your friends and family might be.

Spend at least 2-3 days on this process. This step is really important!

Find a Great Cover Designer

Your cover is the other *really* important factor for driving readers to your book page. If they don't like your cover, they won't click on it, and if they can't read your title on a small thumbnail, they will ignore it altogether.

Unless you are a professional designer, do NOT create your own cover, tempting as it may be. And no, the "Cover Creator" provided in KDP or CreateSpace is not a great option either - if you want a professional looking cover that is.

There is a technique to creating winning eBook covers - those that SELL. It's not really important whether you love your cover or find it artistic and beautiful. Its main and only purpose is to get people to *click* on it!

To get them through the door.

That's all it's for - and it is incredibly important for that purpose.

When you are new to eBook publishing, it is best to trust experienced designers who know what sells and what the winning traits of successful book covers are.

It may not always be what you would personally prefer, but you want it to sell, right?

Once again, you could offer a job on Upwork, but you would need to clarify that you require experience in eBook covers, and you would want to see samples from bestselling book covers they created.

I would suggest two other options and I especially like the first:

99 Designs

This is a really cool platform allowing you to hold a contest among designers from all around the world.

You give a brief outline of your book and include a mock up and any specifics that are important to you (preferred fonts, colors, photos, etc.).

With this information, a number of designers from all around the world will get to work and submit a design for your consideration.

3

Launch your contest

We share your design contest with our community of more than 1126,000 designers. Buyer Seller is like like professional designers will brainstorm ideas just for you.

Beard & Comb

4

Receive dozens of designs
—

You can then choose the one you like best and if you don't like any you get your money back - no risk!

It's fun and it's awesome to see different ideas and options - and you have a choice.

The contest costs $299 - again fully refundable if you don't like any of the designs - and you will most likely walk away with a fantastic cover.

100Covers

The sister company of Buckbooks and expert cover designers for ebooks. If you want to book a Buckbooks promo as a brand new author with no reviews, this will be your best chance of getting in.

Book covers start at $100

Let your Social Media followers decide

Many cover designers will provide you with 2 possible design options - and of course, 99 Designs with a whole list of options.

Once you pick your two favorites, share the options on your social media and ask your friends' and followers' to pick their favorite.

It will get them engaged and interested in your book launch - and they will be more objective than you are and might even provide some valuable feedback.

Or - once again - you can use Pickfu.

Build your Author Website

Once you have chosen your title and while your editor and cover designer are at work, you can use the time to set up an author's website.

This is a very important promotional tool and you should have one from the first book you publish.

A website serves two purposes:

1) A virtual business card and press kit

2) A landing page to collect your reader's email addresses for list building

The Importance of a List

Owning your own mailing list of devoted readers is an important and very powerful marketing tool.

In fact, email marketing is considered the most effective marketing strategy, even more than Google and Facebook Ads together.

What's more - you own it. No one can take it from you, unlike social media or even Amazon who could suspend your account or change their rules at any time.

A mailing list allows you to keep in touch with your readers, alert them of new releases, invite them to become reviewers and even build a business around your books.

As we discussed in the opening chapter, Kindle Publishing can bring many wonderful benefits aside from just publishing a book and generating extra income:

- Being a published author **instantly makes you an authority in your field** - even more so as a bestselling author!

- If your books sell well, they will provide a **constant stream of new clients and customers for whatever business or service you are running**. People will be naturally interested and trust you, because you already proved that you know "your stuff" and can help them.

- Because of this, Kindle Publishing can also be **a fantastic List builder**.

All of this on auto-pilot!

Amazon actually *pays you* to build your list, get new customers and become an authority in your field - how awesome is that?!

However, you will waste all those amazing benefits, if you don't have a way to connect with readers beyond your book.

How will they contact you if you don't have a website?

How can you get them on your mailing list if you don't have one?

See where I'm going....?

So, in order to not waste that wonderful opportunity, you can spend the next few days setting up a basic website.

Here is how:

Step 1 - Go with Wordpress

That's what most successful marketers and authors use these days. It's easy to set up and similar to working on Microsoft Word.

You need a self-hosted blog - not a freebie site like Blogger, Weebly or Wordpress.COM - which is not to be confused with the awesome free software Wordpress.ORG, which is what we are going for.

You can easily get excellent hosting for under $5 a month and **this link will give a great discount on a top rated hosting service, so you can start at just $3.49 a month**!

It takes 3 minutes to sign up, and then you can start getting your site ready.

Book #1 of this series can quickly get you up and running with a new Wordpress website - the sassy way....;-)

Or - if you want it even faster - you can watch **this video - "Build a Blog or Website in 10 Minutes"** *(see Resources Page)*.

Your Domain Name

You will need to choose a domain name = YourAwesomeWebsite.com

If you plan on only one book, use your book title as your domain name. In the above example, a possible domain name could be *StartingABlog.com* - That name is probably taken, so you would have to find a variation, possibly adding your name or brand name:

StartingABlogTheSassyWay.com - or
StartingABlogWithNOClue.com - you get the idea....

Try to not make the name too long.

If you plan to write more than one book, you could pick your name, plus "author", as a domain name. Or the series name.

Always try to include a relevant keyword to help with ranking in Google - or other search engines.

If you already have a website, even better, then you should include a book page.

What to put on your Author Website?

A simple website could start with just the following pages:

HOME PAGE with
- Book cover
- Book Synopsis
- Buy now Button
(you can use your book's Amazon affiliate link on your website, but *never* in your Kindle books - absolutely not allowed! - outside affiliate links are ok in Kindle)

AUTHOR PAGE WITH A BIO
- Short (250 words) and long version
- Nice photo also downloadable
- Book cover downloadable

Don't stress about downloadable if that's too complicated during your 30 days. You can always add that later

REVIEWS, BLURBS, TESTIMONIALS

BOOK EXCERPT (Optional)

CONTACT PAGE

Again, keep it simple in the beginning, you can always add more later, or get some help on Fiverr to add more complex features.

If all this feels too complicated, you can outsource the set up to **Fiverr** but *first*, you need to **sign up for hosting and a domain name** *(see Resources page for the link)*.

An experienced web designer/Wordpress expert should easily be able to set this up for you in 1 hour. But they will need your hosting information, the two sets of login info that you will receive during sign up, before they can begin.

Setting up a Landing Page

A landing page will be the place where you collect people's email addresses. To entice them to click over, you will add a free offer at the beginning (and/or end) of your book.

This can be an interesting free report, ebook, cheat sheet or checklist related to your book. Doesn't have to be long, but should be information that is helpful to your readers. Something they would *really* want. You may have to play around with this a little, if you don't get any sign ups. Just try a different Freebie until you find something that works.

With the "right" freebie, people will gladly click on the link, give their email address and then get your free offer. Checklists and Cheat sheets related to your book topic tend to work really well and are easy and quick to set up.

If you want to see what a landing page looks like, just click on the link on the first page to **get your free Kindle Publishing 30 Day Planner**….;-)

For this, I used a paid tool named Thrive Content Builder, but you can start with a free plugin, aptly named **Wordpress Landing Pages**.

You can find the link, which includes an instructional video on the Resources Page.

Sign up with a Mailing list Provider

To collect all the emails from your landing page, you need to connect that page with a mailing list provider who will store the addresses in lists that you can then send emails to - or set up auto-responders.

The two most commonly used options are:

- Aweber

- Mailchimp - Free for the first 2000 subscribers, BUT no auto-responder or automation features. You would have to upgrade to the paid version. However, if you don't want to overwhelm yourself with too many expenses right now, this can be a good and easy start.

If tech stuff is not your strength, once again, just hire someone on Fiverr for a few bucks to set this up for you. AWeber also has fantastic customer support and will go out of their way to help you with this.

Final Edits & Formatting

By now, you should have received you manuscript back from your editor and can now implement any suggested changes.

Also, be sure to check feedback from your test readers and apply as necessary. Read through your manuscript a few more times and then export as a Word doc or ePub.

Add a Review Request

This is really important and best done on a separate page at the end of your book, right after your final chapter.

Just 1-3 sentences thanking the reader for buying your book and reading it all the way to the end. Then ask them a small favor: If they have a moment, could they please leave a review. Don't forget to add the direct link to your Amazon book page once it's published sometime next week.

Mention how helpful feedback is for you, also for future books and thank them once again.

I'm paraphrasing, because it's best if you use your own style and language.

Add your Freebie

This is the other important part to add. Either in the beginning or at the end, add a page titled "Free Bonus" "Your free Gift" or similar, write a quick introduction and then add a link to your landing page where readers can enter their email address to access the free report or whatever you are offering.

You should also mention the Bonus once or twice throughout the text since Amazon usually sets "SRL" = the place where the eReader will open for the first time - to Chapter 1, *not* the intro or prior pages.

Plus, sometimes people forget or aren't ready yet, so, it's good to give several opportunities to download.

The next important step will now be to properly format your book....

Formatting your eBook

Kindle books used to be limited to .MOBI files while most other eBook platforms used ePUB.

This has changed now and you can upload a wide variety of different file types, from .doc/.docx (Word), html, ePUB and a few others.

The Resources page has specifications of each file type according to KDP.

I usually use ePUB, which you can easily export from both Scrivener and Word, but you should always test how it looks on the different devices by using one of these to apps:

Kindle Gen
Kindle Previewer

If everything looks good, you are ready to upload your file. If not, you might want to hire someone on **Fiverr** to finalize the formatting for you.

It's important to keep file size under 3MB - otherwise, you will not be allowed to set your price to 0.99 cents. This would only be the case if you have a lot of images or other large files in your book. In that case, be sure to downsize before adding them to your document.

You can also use **Calibre** - a free software - to quickly transfer your file to .MOBI. That sometimes lowers file size enough to be under the 3 MB threshold.

Otherwise, once again, outsource to someone who is experienced with this. It's not worth spending endless hours trying to figure out tech stuff. There are more important things to focus on before your launch and plenty of inexpensive Fiverr gigs that can help you with this. Just make sure they have a large number of 5 star reviews and a fast turnaround.

Chapter 7 - WEEK 4: Pre-Launch

You are almost at the finish line, just a few more days - and it's Launch Day!!

In Week 4 - Pre-Launch Week - you will first of all create an account with KDP and upload your book. Then follow up with your promos and reviewers and finally, set up your Author Central Page, which is your dedicated Author page on Amazon.

Let's begin!

What is KDP?

"KDP" stands for "Kindle Direct Publishing" and is Amazon's platform for uploading and managing all Kindle portfolios.

You first need to create an account using your regular Amazon login info and you can set that up here:

KDP.Amazon.com

It's pretty self-explanatory and once your account is created you will land on this page, your publishing dashboard or "Bookshelf" as it is called:

All your books will be listed here and if you click on "Reports" right next to "Bookshelf" (at the top), you can see your daily sales per book and earnings per country.

To create a new title, click on the tab next to the horizontal red arrow: "Create a New Title" -> + "Kindle eBook".

This gets you into your new eBook's backend. Most of it is self-explanatory. Just one word of caution - make sure the title and subtitle you enter matches exactly what's on your cover.

This is a new restriction. In the past, authors frequently used the subtitle field to place extra keywords - including famous author names and book titles - without them ever being on the cover, all just to to game Amazon's algorithm. That, however, is no longer allowed and Amazon enforces this quite fiercely.

You will get an email with a warning to remove any additional text that's not on your cover within 5 days or your book will be removed.

Even on the cover, however, you are not allowed to mention other author names or titles.

Next, you can enter your author name, and then you will see the following 3 fields that will determine your long term success -> whether your book will rank or not, and therefore, whether people can find you on Amazon to buy your book:

Description - Amazon Keywords - Categories

Let's start with the description:

Book Description

Writing a high converting book description entails three areas:

1) SEO
2) Copywriting
3) Formatting

SEO

Treat your description like a blog post that you want to rank in Google, because that's exactly what you want to do - that - and, of course, show up high in Amazon searches.

This means you need to optimize your description for SEO, e.g. your chosen keywords (remember week 1?).

Your description needs to be long enough for the Amazon and Google bots to take notice and "index" your book page. "Indexing" means, your page and every word on it is properly catalogued within the algorithm that can then use that information to properly rank your book.

If "ranking" and "SEO" (= how to rank in Google) are completely new to you, I once again suggest reading **Book #3 of the series,** a quick 2 hour read that will get you up to speed on all things SEO. Basics that anyone marketing on the Internet needs to know - .....and as a publisher, you have now also become an internet marketer!

Try to write at least 500 words and sprinkle all your keywords throughout the text. It should sound natural, no keyword stuffing, but if possible, try to mention them all at least once. Your main keyword 3-5 times. Again, where it fits naturally. It needs to be pleasant and fun to read.

Copywriting

Copywriting is the art of using the right words and combination of words to entice consumers to buy.

Well written copy can make a huge difference in conversion rates, and for your description you need to once again put on your marketer's hat.

To get some ideas, browse through the top ranking book descriptions for your topic. See what they write and what triggers they use to get readers to buy. How do you respond to each? And what is it that sets the great ones apart? Find one that really "nails it" in your opinion and use it as a model.

It doesn't even have to be from your own topic. It can be something related. This is more about the structure and certain triggers than the exact content.

Obviously, don't copy anyone else's description, but it's perfectly fine to use the overall structure as a template and then craft your own awesome description.

Use a few power words where applicable - *find an extensive list on the Resources Page* - and use short paragraphs and frequent sub heads (H2s) to make it easy to read and skim through.

If you know your reader's problem, start with that and explain how your book can help solve it.

Go into detail about the different chapters, use bullet points and give readers a really good sense of what they can expect.

Also, clear up any misconceptions - what your book does *not* cover - to avoid disappointing readers who will then leave angry reviews.

End with a call to action like:

Scroll to the top of the page and select the BUY button.

Formatting

Amazon allows some basic html formatting for the description. It used to include colors, the famous Amazon orange, but now that's only available on the Author Central page.

You can set up headlines, sub headings, bold, italics and a number of other options.

No worries, you don't need to know any coding. Just write your description in a normal text editor or MS Word and add the following start and end tags as needed (notice that the end tag always has a /):

<H1>use this for headlines</H1>
<H2>use this for sub heads. On the author page, this will also turn orange</H2>
use this if you want your text bold
use this if you want your text in italics
<u>use this to underline text</u>

The Resources Page features a link to an awesome Amazon Book Description Generator to automatically set up html tags - and - an example of a well written book description to help you get started.

You can also hire someone to write a winning book description *for* you. **Archangel Ink** offers this service as part of their editing/proofreading package.

Keywords & Categories

The next two areas are "Keywords" and "Categories".

If you did your research in chapter 1, this should be pretty easy.

Please note: The 7 keywords, you can enter here are considered internal "Amazon Keywords". They are not the same as the "SEO keywords" you use in your book's description and title to trigger the search algorithm of *both* Amazon and Google.

Google and other search engines do not have access to these 7 internal keywords and their importance for ranking wanes over time. That's why you need to optimize your book page first and foremost, so that your book shows up high in searches for months and years to come.

Of course, both keyword types can overlap, but Amazon, once again, has specific rules of what you can and cannot use in these 7 tabs:

- No information that is covered somewhere else in your book such as title, category, etc.
- No claim about quality like "best" or "top"
- No Statements that are temporary like "on sale", "new", or "limited offer"
- No common information "book", "ebook", "kindle"
- No Misspellings to game the system, unless it is a translation issue like "Mao Zedong" and "Mao Tse-tung"
- No Variations of words or spacing
- Anything that is misleading

I've never seen anyone getting punished for using their main keyword in both the title and 7 Amazon keywords, but technically we are not supposed to do that and it's probably just a question of time until they start cracking down on this, too, but for now I wouldn't worry too much.

Just pick 7 from your list of 15 keywords. Those that you find most important and enter them one by one. Again, keywords are not just one or two words, but usually phrases of 3+ words. The more specific you are, the easier it will be to rank - as long as those phrases have a decent monthly search volume.

If you need a refresher, please go back to Chapter 4.

Now lets look at:

Categories

You get to choose 2 and unfortunately, they don't match what you see on Amazon, so in most cases, you will have to contact customer service to have them manually place your book into a specific sub category.

How to select categories?

For launch week - when you want to rank as a bestseller, and possibly even #1 - you want to pick 1 category that's easy to rank, where most other books have a high Sales Rank, ideally over 30K. A few below is fine, you will still be a bestseller, but a category with most books under 10K could be difficult, at least for #1 ranking.

Even when using paid promos like Buckbooks, number of sales will still very much depend on reader interest in your topic. While you can never predict how high your Sales Rank will go during launch week, 20s or even 10s will usually not be a problem, especially if you have a great cover and title

For the 2nd category, pick one that's a little more competitive -> has more active sales -> therefore can generate more downloads and momentum for your book, even if your placement will be lower on that bestseller list.

In this case, you want to look for the following parameters among the top 20 (no exact science, just as a rough estimate):

1-3 books under 5K

1-5 books under 10K

A minimum of 10 books under 30K

That means the majority of books in that category have regular daily sales.

Those numbers aren't always exact and they don't need to be, but can give you a good overall sense.

Use **KindleSpy** - or do it manually - and browse through all related sub categories (always use the final end thread, the most niched down category) and make a list of possible candidates.

You need more than two, because sometimes a category isn't working well or suddenly another book is placed there that pushes yours further down. Also, over time, the numbers change and you will occasionally need to switch categories, especially when your book sales are stagnating.

Another thing to consider is spreading the categories over two different genres, if applicable. For example, internet marketing could be placed under both Business and Computers and you spread your net much wider that way.

Not required - and not always applicable - but something to keep in mind.

Publish or Pre-order

At the bottom of page 1 you are given the option to either publish right away or make your book available for pre-order.

With pre-order your book will already show on Amazon and people can buy it, but it won't be added to their account until launch day.

Pre-order can be a nice way to create some buzz and schedule promos who often require an ASIN (=Amazon's "ISBN" for Kindle books), but your launch day needs to be at least 4 days away and your final book and cover files need to be uploaded 3 days (72 hours) before launch, which I always found a little limiting.

If you are on a tight schedule - and you will be on this 30 day itinerary - it's better to have more flexibility and make changes until launch day.

Officially, it takes up to 72 hours for a new book to show - or any updates thereafter - but in practice it's usually just a few hours, though there have been rare cases of technical issues within Amazon where things got backed up for several days, so best not to plan on last minute, but normally - in most cases - a day before should be enough (*most* times.....).

Another important fact to know about pre-order: if you change or cancel/unpublish your book, your pre-order rights will be suspended for a full year! So you need to be 100% sure that you can keep your launch date.

Uploading your Content

On the next page you get to upload your content: your ePub or Word file and your cover.

First, you need to enable Digital Rights Management - click "Yes". This prevents unauthorized distribution of your book.

Next, you can upload your book file & cover:

At the bottom you can once again use the previewer function to make sure everything looks good.

Also, always check that all links are working.

Now you are ready to move on to page 3:

KDP Select - Should you...?

At the top of page 3 you will be given the option to sign up for KDP Select.

Just click on "Visit the Promotions Page" and you will get to this screen:

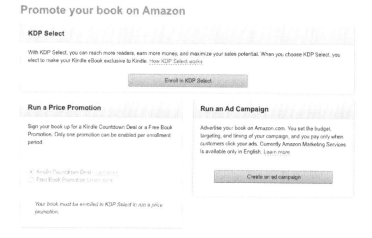

This is also where you set up ad campaigns which we'll talk about in the final chapter.

What is KDP Select?

If you choose to enroll your book in KDP Select you agree to be exclusive with Amazon for the next 90 days. That means you cannot sell your book anywhere else - not on your website (though you can certainly link to Amazon), not on Barnes & Noble, Kobo or iBooks.

After 90 days, you can either leave or renew.

Why would you agree to exclusivity?

Well....because KDP offers some great promo options that will be helpful, especially as a brand new author:

- Countdown Deals

- Free Promos

It is the latter that we are most interested in - the FREE Promo.

I already explained why free promos are so powerful and why - for your first book - I strongly recommend you use them, for at least 2-3 days.

As a new author you want to get your first book in front of as many people as possible and the difference between a FREE promo and 99c can easily be between thousands vs. hundreds of downloads depending on your book topic and the promos you use.

The only way you can do a free promo is by enrolling in KDP Select, so that pretty much answers that question for you.

If you don't ever want to run any free promos, no need to enroll, but if you *do* want to leverage the awesome power of FREE, you need to be enrolled.

Just make sure you uncheck the automatic renewal box - here is how:

Click on the gray tab on the right and in the pop up choose KDP Select Info:

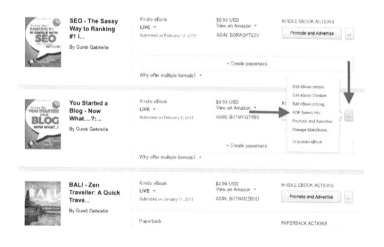

Then click on "Manage KDP Select Enrollment":

Uncheck the box for automatic renewal and save (don't forget that part!):

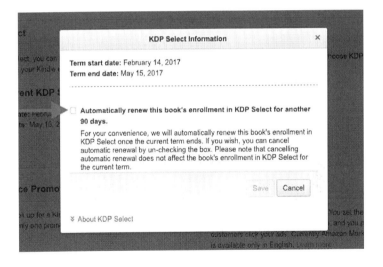

You get 5 FREE days per 90 day period and this is how you can schedule them:

Scroll down on the same page to "Run a Price Promotion" and select "Free Book Promotion". Then click "Create a new Free Book Promotion".

Run a Price Promotion

Sign your book up for a Kindle Countdown Deal or a Free Book Promotion. Only one promotion can be enabled per enrollment period.

○ Kindle Countdown Deal Learn more
◉ Free Book Promotion Learn more

Create a new Free Book Promotion

On the next screen you enter your dates and the screen will also show you how many free days you have already used and how many you have left.

Create a new Free Book Deal

Choose when the promotion will start and end

Kindle Free Book Deal promotions can run for up to 5 days.

Start Date: _____   End Date: _____

Free promotion days used: 4 / 5

Click on the date box and a little calendar will pop up where you can select your dates.

That's it!

At the end of the last promo day, the price will automatically go back to whatever regular price you have set.

To create greater urgency, you can set your regular price a little higher - like $4.99 or even $9.99, because the regular price will still show on Amazon while the book is free and it looks a lot more enticing when you get a higher priced book for free.

If you intend to switch to 0.99 right after your free promo - which I would recommend to get your bestseller ranking - you need to switch the price to 0.99 at least 1 day before the 99c promo start date - which in this case would be during your Free Promo dates.

With any updates it can theoretically take up to 72 hours though it's more likely to be just a few hours or a day - just plan enough time, because if the book is not properly priced at 99c when that promo starts, the promo services will be quite upset and might not ever allow you to promote with them again. Or they might just remove your book from the promo altogether without a refund.

Therefore, if you want to play it safe and not stress over it during launch week, just set your regular price at $0.99 and you won't have to change anything until later during launch week.

Now let's look at how you actually set up pricing:

Pricing & Royalties

This is really easy:

First, you select "All territories" and then click on "All Marketplaces" to open tabs for the international stores.

There is no reason not to make your book available everywhere, and the system will automatically convert prices for you. For Euro, CAN, AUD, and British Pound, I usually keep the same amount as for USD, e.g. 0.99, 2.99, 3.99 etc., but that's up to you.

An interesting feature is "KDP Pricing Support". It shows you what other books with the same topic have

charged on average - in this case \$2.99 - the most widely available Kindle price:

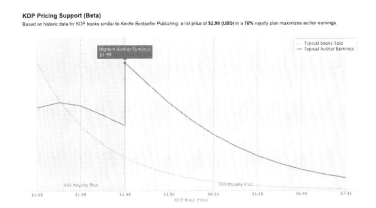

This is just a suggestion, but it's certainly helpful to know what customers usually expect to pay for this type of book.

Next, you select a royalty rate - once again:

- less than $2.99 & more than $9.99 = 35%

- anything between $2.99-$9.99 = 70%

Then you enter your prices for all stores and you are done.

I would suggest enabling Matchbook. This allows people who buy the print version of your book to get the Kindle version at a reduced rate or free.

Lending allows customers to lend your book to friends or family once for up to 14 days. During this time, the book will not be available to the lender. All books are automatically enrolled and you can only turn this feature off at the 35% rate.

I usually leave it enabled, but it's a personal choice.

Finally, you need to accept KDP's Terms and click "Publish".

That's it!

You are now officially a Published Author!

Congratulations!!

Checking Bestseller Rank and Categories

It will usually take a few hours for your book to pass through review, and you will be notified by email once your book is available in the Amazon store.

That's when you want to take note of your ASIN number - Amazon's version of an ISBN for Kindle books - and your book url.

You can see your ASIN by scrolling down your book page:

Product Details

File Size: 1656 KB
Print Length: 100 pages
Simultaneous Device Usage: Unlimited
Publisher: A SassyZenGirl Guide (November 2, 2015)
Publication Date: November 2, 2015
Sold by: Amazon Digital Services, Inc.
Language: English
ASIN: B017ID54G6
Text-to-Speech: Enabled
X-Ray: Not Enabled
Word Wise: Not Enabled
Lending: Enabled
Enhanced Typesetting: Enabled
Amazon Best Sellers Rank: #1,493 Paid in Kindle Store (See Top 100 Paid in Kindle Store)
      #1 in Kindle Store > Kindle Short Reads > Two hours or more (65-100 pages) > **Education & Reference**
      #1 in Kindle Store > Kindle eBooks > Education & Teaching > Teacher Resources > **Professional Development**
      #1 in Kindle Store > Kindle eBooks > Computers & Technology > **Web Site Design**

Right underneath will be your Sales Rank = "Amazon Best Seller Rank" for the entire Kindle store - and then your rank within your chosen categories.

The 3 best categories will show here, including "Book" ranking (=Print) and "Kindle Short Reads" if your book is under 100 pages. The rest can be found at the bottom of your book page - just scroll down.

It's the ranking in these 3 categories that you will want to watch during launch week. That's where you become a Bestseller - and possibly even #1.

To see your book on the Bestseller pages, just click on the final sub category, and it will lead you straight to the corresponding Bestseller page. In the above example that would be "Education & Reference", "Professional Development", or "Web Site Design".

This was my very first book and in all 3 categories it had reached #1, including Kindle Short Reads. This was before I had even added the print version. Otherwise, that would show here as well.

Even better, the book also reached #1 in the *overall* Education category:

Sometimes, Amazon places you in additional categories that they think your book is relevant for, so you might see categories, you hadn't even asked for - or an overall category as in the above case.

It's fun once the momentum gets going during launch week….;-)

When your book is first published, you probably won't see any numbers yet, because your book needs at least one sale (or first download in the free lists) to trigger the algorithm.

So download/buy your book, open it and check that everything looks ok. If you notice any problems, correct them and re-upload the file.

It usually takes a few hours for Sales/Bestseller rank to update, so just check back later.

Make sure that the correct sub categories are listed. Since categories in your KDP backend are not the same as Amazon categories, you will often have to contact customer service and have them place it there.

This can take another day or two to complete - so plan at least 3-4 days between your first publish - = your pre-launch - and your official launch date.

Even a full week is fine, but I wouldn't do more, because during the first 28 days, Amazon will promote you in the "Hot New Releases" section on the right.

If you are a bestseller, your book will constantly show there during those 28 days - which is free - and very effective - advertising! - so you don't want to loose too many days on pre-launch.

Set up Free Promo Days

Next, you want to schedule your free promo days. Go back to your KDP back end, click on Promotions, then Free Promotions and enter the dates.

If you are worried about switching in time to 99c during launch week, just set your regular price to 99c and you won't have to do anything - though your free promo will look more tempting if the book is higher priced.

You should also schedule 1 free day *before* launch day, so your reviewers can download the book for free and leave their reviews as "verified", which is very important.

KDP Support

One additional step I highly recommend during pre-launch is setting up phone support.

You can always contact KDP support by clicking on the tiny "Contact" link at the bottom of the page. This will open the following window:

You can choose one of the options and send a message. It usually takes about 24 hours for a response, so not exactly fast when you are in the midst of launch week and need something corrected quickly.

This is why you should send them a message during pre-launch and ask for phone support to be enabled. Ask for 2 weeks and given them an end date. They usually do it without problem and then you see that option activated on the very same contact page.

Just click the phone button and they will call you right back (during regular business hours).

With email support I've had mixed experiences. Simple things like connecting print and Kindle versions always gets done without problem, but with other issues you often have to ask for a supervisor - and you have to mention that in the opening line, ideally with SUPERVISOR in caps, or they might not see it and just send you a generic reply.

Since it always takes a day for them to get back, I usually switch to supervisor when it doesn't get done the first time - and they are mostly superb.

It's a huge worldwide organization, so you will occasionally encounter these problems. During launch week though, and even a few days before - when things can get a little hectic - you definitely want phone support enabled...

Your Author Central Page

Once your book is published, Amazon will create an author page for you. It usually takes a few days and you can sign up and check here:

AuthorCentral.Amazon.com

Once inside, enter your name in the search function and when you see it come up, you can "add" your book if it isn't already showing.

The Author Central team will check the veracity of your claim, which can take another day or so - and then you are good to go.

You should add a few nice pictures and a bio. The bio will also show on your book page.

In addition, you can add your social media links, videos and your blog feed.

And….you can add "Editorial Reviews" if you have any from newspapers, other authors, top reviewers etc. Those will appear above your bio (on your book page) and can make quite a difference in sales.

You can also mention them in your book description to make sure people see them.

Among the really amazing features on the Author Central Page are the analytics.

They will show you (over time) your all-time bestseller ranking, where most of your readers come from (on a map), sales numbers etc.

A really great section, definitely check it out sometime - though it will be mostly empty in the beginning, of course…..;-)

Setting up your author page is really important, because interested readers often check it out.

On the Resources Page you can find an article that goes in-depth on how to create a great Author Central Page.

Finalize Promos & Reviews

Don't forget to add your book link to the "Review Request" page at the end of your book and then upload/publish again.

You will probably have to re-upload your book a few times before launch day, because there are usually a few corrections, additions, links not working etc.

Also, add the book link to your website and add reviews as they come in.

Keep building the buzz on all your social media, friends, family, colleagues, mailing list, forums, Facebook groups, Reddit threads, Goodreads. Anywhere you can possibly mention your book - Do it! - And spread the excitement!!

You can also add a press release, schedule interviews with relevant newspapers, blogs, podcasts, and local TV stations - whatever can help spread the word about your book. Guest posts during launch week can also be very powerful.

Click here to find out how you can land first rate Guest Posts on Top Online Magazines and Blogs:

SassyZenGirl.com/Guest-Blogging

You can also post daily short excerpts on Facebook and invite comments and feedback.
Anything you can do to build buzz and get people excited for your book!

Final Check on your Promos

Check in once more with all your promos and forward them your book link if you haven't already.

If you set up guest posts, check in with the blog owner, confirm the dates again and send them your book link, so they can add it to the post.

Same with any press or podcast appearances you may have scheduled. Check in and forward your book link, so they can all add it to their website.

Schedule your Reviewers

Let your reviewers know that they can now leave a review.

For this, you should do another - private - Free promo day or 2 - so your reviewers can access the book for free and can then leave a review from within their account (remind them to be logged in when they leave a review). That way, their review will count as a "verified", which counts a lot more and is also more trustworthy to readers.

Remind them once again of the review guidelines, so their reviews won't get deleted a few weeks down the road. I have seen it several times. It does really happen - and to many authors - so prepare your reviewers properly and make it easy for them.

Reviews should first and foremost be helpful to a potential buyer and provide detailed, specific information about the book and why they liked it. How it helped them, etc.

A review should never address you personally or thank you or tell people what a great person you are (those will get deleted), but offer the customer a really helpful - and objective - feedback.

That's pretty much it for Pre-.launch Week!

Chapter 8 - Launch Week

During Launch week, you have only two tasks:

1) Promote, promote, promote!

2) Watch your Bestseller rank every few hours and see yourself rise to the top!

That's it!

The hard work is behind you and while you should spend every free minute promoting, this part should be really fun.

Don't forget to enjoy it....;-)

It's an awesome feeling once you realize that you have become - and can now call yourself - a:

"Bestselling Author"

If you applied what was taught so far, got some powerful promotions going and placed yourself in the right categories - this should be an awesome week for you.

Still continue to promote your book as much as possible and invite your friends, family and colleagues to spread the word as well, especially during the 99c phase, which many will see as a great bargain.

Be sure to share your Bestseller screenshots. People will be excited and happy for you - and be even more enthusiastic to share your book link.

Success breeds more success and it will also be rewarding for all those who helped in the process, like your reviewers, test readers etc. Be sure to thank them and share your joy with them.

Sales Rank updates

As for ranking - please note that sales numbers and sales rank are updated with at least a few hours delay - easily 12 hours.

If you don't see your book moving even though you have promotions running, don't panic, just wait. Check once at the top of the hour and gradually, you will start seeing some movement.

You can always check in your KDP backend under "Reports" how many books have already been downloaded (green for free, and red for sales) though that, too, is posted with some delay.

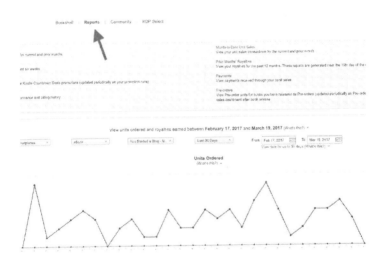

Otherwise, keep an eye on your price changes (from free to 99c) and switch to your regular price as soon as the last 99c promo is completed to take advantage of the promo momentum.

What is considered a "Bestseller"?

Well...there is no specific number. I usually consider anything in the top 10 of a sub category a "Bestseller", even the top 20 - and anyone making it into the Top 100 in the overall Kindle store or one of the major categories like "Business" or "Self Help".

According to Amazon, you can call yourself a "Bestselling Author" if your book is listed in the top 100 of any category or sub category!

When you scroll down on the bestseller page, you will see this:

If you sell even just a few books, it is almost impossible *not* to be a Bestseller in one of the small sub categories, that's why there are many Kindle Publishing courses guaranteeing you a Bestseller for a substantial course fee....

I always strive for the #1 spot, because that also comes with the "#1 Bestseller Badge" - but at the very least the Top 10 of a sub category. I wouldn't call myself a bestselling author otherwise, but that's just me.

Does Free Ranking count as Bestseller status?

Yes, technically it does, at least according to Amazon. There are 2 bestseller lists for each category and while a free book is not really "sold", it does count as a bestseller:

Again, it's a personal choice. While the top spots in the free bestseller lists can also be very competitive and it's exciting to see your book there for the first time - definitely enjoy that moment! - I would not in good conscience call myself a "Bestselling Author" when all I have to show are free downloads, not an actual paid sale.

Again, that's just me, there are no fixed rules, but that's the best answer I have for the "What's a Bestseller" question.

Either way - once you hit bestseller status, and maybe even #1 - don't forget to celebrate!!

Becoming a "Bestselling Author" is an awesome - epic - moment in your life!

Really take time to enjoy it!

Chapter 9 - Post-Launch

What's next?

Definitely, keep promoting your book. Mention it in your email signature with a direct link and also on your website and social media.

Whenever you guest post or appear on podcasts or other interviews, mention your book with a direct link to the Amazon sale's page.

If your book lends itself to a series, start writing the next…

Add more Books

Kindle publishing becomes lucrative once you have a number of books, ideally in a series. If people like one book, they will usually buy your other books, too.

Also, the newer books still benefit from "Hot New Releases" exposure, which tends to increase sales for your older books as well. Plus, they often show in the "also bought" section.

If you want to build a long term income with Kindle Publishing, try to publish a new book every 2 months for at least a year or two. With each new book your income will grow and they all help sell each other.

If you have an easily recognizable cover template, people will start noticing your brand over time and will be more motivated to check out some of your books, even if they were skeptical at first.

Add more Reviews

Keep adding reviews as much as possible. Keep contacting top reviewers, remind your new subscribers on occasion, network on Goodreads, etc.

Amazon has openly stated on many occasions that reviews are one of their most important ranking factors (number and star rating), so you can never have too many.

Also, be generous with reviews for other books and products you buy on Amazon. Now that you know how important they are, try to make it a point to *always* leave a review when you buy something on Amazon.

Help others and others will help you. Not necessarily the same people, but generosity tends to attract more and it doesn't take long to write a review.

Promos

Once a month run a promo for one of your books - or several days of promo, especially if sales start slacking.

One book picking up momentum usually also helps your other books and by rotating them on a monthly basis, promo audiences won't get tired of seeing the same book over and over.

Amazon Ads

Amazon ads are a newer feature, but are beginning to see some nice returns for Kindle books. That is - if they are set up correctly. In that way, they are similar to Facebook Ads. Unless you know how to properly set up campaigns, you will probably just spend money with little return.

A brand new course by Derek Doepker solves this problem and can help boost your sales long term.

Add Print & Audio

Most importantly, add the following two platforms to your portfolio to increase visibility - and most of all, sales:

Add a Print Edition

From my own experience, I can strongly recommend adding print versions to each of your books as soon as possible.

In some cases - like my **Bali book** - print sales far outsell Kindle. I'm stunned every month when I see the numbers.

It depends on the type of book - some are really popular in print and others are not at all - but you should have both options available. It's free money once uploaded....

Amazon offers print-on-demand services through **Createspace** and it's free to set up and submit a book (if you use a Createspace ISBN).

KDP is also now in the process of offering print services, which would allow you to have all your versions in one place.

I like Createspace because they pay royalties after 30 days - Kindle after 60 - but both are good options.

Set up and submission are pretty self-explanatory. The main difference to eBook submissions is that you need to pick a specific size (dimensions) and then adjust your cover accordingly.

Setting up the interior book file can be quite time consuming, but you can easily outsource that process.

Once your print book shows in the Amazon store, you need to contact KDP and ask them to connect both your Kindle and Print versions. They usually do it within a day and then both versions show on the same page.

Please note - while you can always make changes to titles and subtitles in KDP, you cannot change your meta data in Createspace, because they are tied to an ISBN which doesn't allow changes to title, author name etc.

You can always change your cover and interior files, as well as description, pricing etc., just not your book's meta data.

Add an Audio Version

Audiobooks have become huge on Amazon and a lot of authors have added audio books to their portfolio with a nice additional income stream.

You can either outsource to places like Archangel Ink (not cheap….) or do it yourself as long as you meet certain audio quality standards.

Derek Doepker has an awesome course to help you record your own audio books - or outsource them at a reasonable rate - and he will personally help and guide you through the process.

Obviously, it is much nicer and more personal for your readers to hear *your* voice rather than a generic voice over artist, but both can work well.

Further Training

While you can absolutely reach Bestseller Status by just applying the principles taught in this book - no further course needed! - some people will prefer one-on-one guidance and an accountability partner, especially if they are not experienced writers or feel overwhelmed by the whole process.

In that case, there is no better training than Chandler Bolt's "Self-Publishing School".

It's a 90 Day course that partners you with an expert coach guiding you through each step along the way and guaranteeing - get this - a:

#1 Amazon Bestseller

Once again, you can absolutely reach #1 by following the strategies taught here, but if it all seems very daunting and you would like a more personal, guided, approach - also on the writing process - this is the Gold Standard among Publishing Courses!

You can start with a series of FREE Training Videos to learn more and can then sign up for the full training if it feels right.

Just click on the link below to get access - the free training will certainly be worth your while - and then you can decide later:

SassyZenGirl.com/Chandler-Bolt

Final Words

There you have it....;-)

A Step-by-Step guide to your first Amazon Bestseller and an in-depth understanding of Amazon's algorithm. Knowledge that you can also apply to your Amazon affiliate sales.

If you are serious about publishing a bestseller, I recommend reading this book a few times, download the **30 Day Bestseller Checklist** and start your Action Plan.

I wish you the best of luck - and much fun with this new adventure!!

Don't forget to celebrate and share a few screenshots when your book shows in the Bestseller lists for the first time!!

Until then I wish you…

Happy Writing & and All the Very Best, Always!

Gundi Gabrielle
aka **SassyZenGirl.com**

A Small Request

Before you go, I'd like to thank you for purchasing this book.

I know you had many guides to choose from, but you took a chance on mine. You rock…;-)

If you found the information helpful and think others might benefit as well, it would be awesome if you could take a brief moment and **leave a review on Amazon**.

This feedback will help me to keep writing books that help you get results. And if you loved it, then please let me know….;-)

Dankeschön & Auf Wiedersehen….

More SassyZenGirl Books:

#1 Bestselling
SUCCESSFUL BLOG Series

BRAND NEW "ZEN TRAVELLER" SERIES

#1 *Bestseller*
ZEN TRAVELLER BALI

Explore the "real" Bali…
the quiet, magical parts
- away from the tourist crowds….

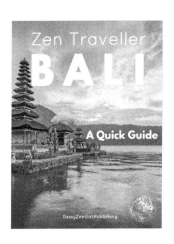

More Zen Traveller guides following soon:
New Zealand, South Africa, Cyprus, Dubai, Namibia among
others…..

About the Author

Gundi Gabrielle is a 5-time #1 Bestselling Author, Internet Entrepreneur and Digital Nomad.

As a former Carnegie Hall conductor and Concert Organist, she decided 3 years ago to make a bold change in her life, packed up a few belongings and drove all the way from Santa Monica, California, to Alaska. She has been traveling ever since and loves exploring this beautiful world without being tied to one place.

She has road tripped through all 50 US States and parts of Canada, lived in several European countries for a number of years and visited most of Europe, as well South America, Southern Africa, Australia, New Zealand and many countries in South East Asia and the Middle East.

She runs the Travel Blog *SassyZenGirl*, writes travel and blogging books and often house or farm sits along her travels, nurturing her love for animals and solitude.

She has no plans of settling down anytime soon…

SassyZenGirl.com

Facebook.com/SassyZenGirl
Instagram.com/SassyZenGirltravels
Youtube.com/c/SassyZenGirl

LuxuryPetCompanion.com

GundiGabrielle.com

Made in the USA
San Bernardino, CA
24 May 2017